Date: 6/2/14

J 793.21 JON
Jones, Jen.
Pampering parties : planning a
party that makes your friends

pampering
PARTIES

Planning a *Party* that Makes Your Friends Say "*Ahhh*"

by Jen Jones

CAPSTONE PRESS
a capstone imprint

Snap Books are published by Capstone Press,
1710 Roe Crest Drive, North Mankato, Minnesota 56003
www.capstonepub.com

Library of Congress Cataloging-in-Publication Data
Jones, Jen.
  Pampering parties : planning a party that makes your friends say "ahhh" / by Jen Jones.
      pages cm. — (Snap books. Perfect parties)
  Summary: "Lots of kids love parties, and this series will help them add to their fun. With plenty of inspiration and information, Perfect Parties includes creative themes, decorating ideas, and party planning tips"-- Provided by publisher.
  ISBN 978-1-4765-4008-5 (library binding)
  ISBN 978-1-4765-6055-7 (eBook PDF)
1. Children's parties—Planning—Juvenile literature. I. Title.

  GV1205.J647 2014
  793.2′1--dc23   2013043738

Editorial Credits
Mari Bolte, editor; Tracy Davies McCabe, designer; Kathy McColley, production specialist;
Sarah Schuette, photo stylist; Sarah Schuette and Marcy Morin, project creators

Photo Credits
Photography by Capstone Studio: Karon Dubke except: Shutterstock: Africa Studio, 14 (middle), 18 (top), Alexander Raths, 24, AlexKol Photography, 26 (top), Ariwasabi, 8 (top left), Baleika Tamara, 27, Christian Bertrand, 20 (middle right), Coprid, 10, cosma, 27 (bottom), Denisa V, 20 (middle left), Diana Taliun, 20 (top), ever, 8 (right bottom), Feng Yu, 8 (top right), Hawk777, 20 (top right), Ipsener, 27 (top), Kesu, cover (right), 14 (top), Loredana Cirstea, 8 (middle), Malivan_Iuliia, 18 (bottom), matka_Wariatka, 19, Matthew Nigel, 26 (bottom), mayamaya, 29, Odua Images, 22, Sea Wave, cover (left), 14 (right), senkaya, 8 (bottom), stockcreations, 13, Tamara Kulikova, 20 (bottom), Teresa Kasprzycka, 25, Valentina Razumova, 27 (middle), Valua Vitaly, cover (middle inset), 14 (bottom), Vankad, 7

Design Elements:
Design Elements by Capstone Studio: Karon Dubke except: Shutterstock: Liv friis-larsen, Victoria Kalinina, Yganko, zsooofija

Printed in the United States of America in Brainerd, Minnesota.
092013   007770BANGS14

TABLE OF CONTENTS

Getting Started

It's not hard to see why people love parties so much. After all, they're festive, fun, and celebrate something that's really important—friendship. The best hostesses throw parties that bring new people together. That's where you come in!

The trick is planning a party that your friends won't forget. Creativity is the key—any interest or hobby can be transformed into a party theme. Get inspired with two unforgettable party ideas. Pamper Me Pretty will get your guests feeling gorgeous and spa-tacular. Tea Time will have them feeling elegantly sweet. First, pick your theme. Then find oodles of ideas for making your party pop!

Of course, it's true that a hostess' work is never done. Endless to-do lists and lots of hands-on tasks often translate to lots of hard work for a hostess. Luckily, it can be a lot of fun—and a lot easier with the right insider intel! The right info can keep you organized, savvy, and sane as you plan your big shindig. Learn ways to cover all of the bases while preparing for your party—and hit a home run with the result.

Save the Date

Soccer practice and dance class and family parties, oh my! With lots of busy schedules to work around (including your own), planning a party often requires a good strategy and a solid plan. Here are some tips to help out with timing:

- Avoid holding your party too close to major holidays. Many of your friends might have a hard time making a shindig on Easter weekend or Thanksgiving. Check the calendar for popular vacation days too, such as Memorial Day or spring break. If you do choose to host a holiday party, make peace with the fact that a few peeps might have to miss out.

- Put your head together with the rest of your family and make sure that there are no scheduling conflicts. If you have a few besties that you can't be without, run the date by them as well.

- Don't forget about Mother Nature! Be sure to have a backup location if you're planning an outdoor party.

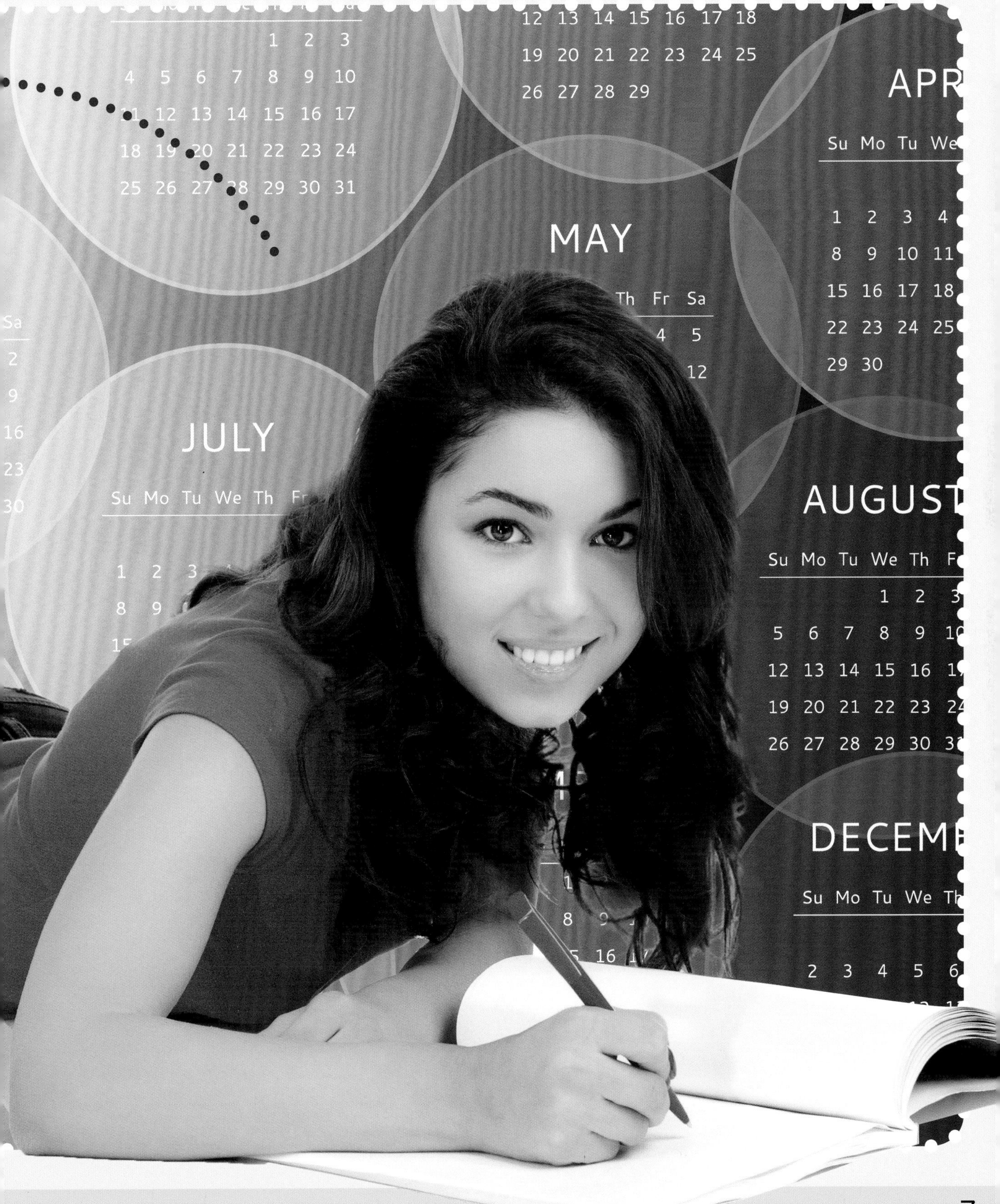
MAY
JULY
AUGUST

Shop 'Til You Drop

Parties are like snowflakes in that no two are alike. However, there are certain staples that almost every hostess needs to throw a successful one. Use this sample shopping list to see what you might need for your shindig. Off to the store you go!

Shopping List

- [ ] paper cups/plates
- [ ] plastic utensils
- [ ] napkins
- [ ] paper towels
- [ ] trash bags
- [ ] 1 pound (455 grams) of ice per person attending. (Plan for twice as much if the party is outdoors.)
- [ ] cleaning supplies
- [ ] tablecloth(s)
- [ ] candles (if celebrating a birthday)
- [ ] thank you notes

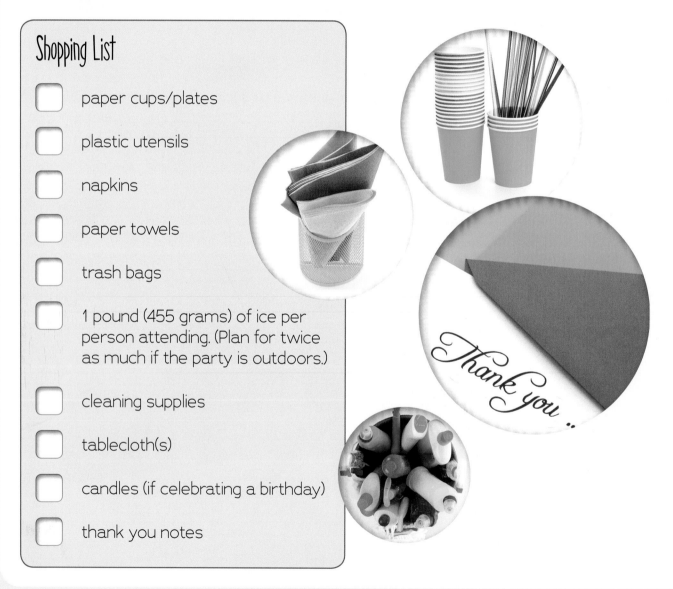

Your food and décor will depend on the menu and other details you decide on. For maximum organization, create a spreadsheet. Make a column for each category.

Fill it with shopping lists for each item. Highlight anything you already have at your house, such as markers and posterboard.

Spa Party Shopping List

Food	Drink	Décor
Polish Puffs: 3 cans colored frosting 2 bags marshmallows 1 bag chocolate chews	**All That Razz:** 2 packs fresh raspberries 4 lemons sparkling water	**Spa Welcome Sign:** posterboard stencil glitter pen markers

Smart Shopper

Want to avoid that "ouch" moment at the cash register? Shop smart! Check to see what you have around the house before your shopping trip. Compare prices online so you have an idea of price range. Dollar stores or thrift stores are also good places to find affordable party goods.

Coupon clipping can also help save some dough. Check out the store's website for printable coupons before heading out to shop. When shopping online, look up coupon codes before you check out. Codes for discounts or free shipping are always nice finds.

Get the Party Started

If your party is starting off with a whimper rather than a bang, no need to call party 9-1-1. Sometimes all you need is a quick kickstart! Icebreaker games are an easy way to melt any tension and to put everyone at ease. Say "so long" to awkward moments with these awesome ideas:

Play The Name Game

Learning everyone's name can sometimes be a tall task. So why not make it more memorable? In this game, each person introduces herself by turning each letter of her name into a silly acronym. The more out-there, the better! Some examples:

Britt = Britt ran into the tater tot
Ashley = Ashley slurps hot lava each year

Share or Dare

Learn more about your guests with a guessing game! Using small sheets of paper, write up a bunch of "shares" and "dares" designed to learn more about your guests. For example, a share could be: "What food completely grosses you out?" A dare could be: "Imitate your fave celeb and have us guess who it is." Place the papers inside colored balloons (using one color for shares and another for dares.) Guests can take turns popping them and playing along!

Fast Track to Fun

Other quickies that are sure to boost the fun factor:

Place game question cards at different points around the party area, inviting your guests to ask each other questions!

Give each guest a bracelet in a single color. Get your guests to trade beads with each other. At the end of the night, each girl should have a rainbow bracelet to take home. Make it a contest, and give a prize to the person with the most colorful bracelet.

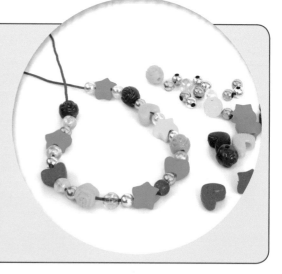

Signature Sips

Ask yourself this question: "If my party was a beverage, what would it be?" The answer just might be your signature sip! Create a beverage that goes perfectly with your party's theme or color scheme. There are plenty of ways to dress up your party drinks.

Rock the Rim

Rimming your beverage glass adds a whole new level of good taste. Moisten the rim of the glass using water, a slice of fruit (such as a lemon, lime, or orange), or chocolate syrup.

Gently dip the rim into a shallow bowl of salt, sugar, or whatever you're using to rim the glass. Let it dry for a moment, then shake any excess off over the sink. Fill your glass with mocktail, and you're good to go!

Make Your Own Sanding Sugar

For an extra twist, decorate your signature sip with custom-colored sanding sugar.

* 1 cup (240 mL) white or sanding sugar
* food coloring
* plastic bag with a seal

1. Place sugar and food coloring in bag. The amount of food coloring you use will depend on how dark you want the sugar to be.

2. Close the top of the bag. Knead until all the sugar is colored. Repeat if the sugar is not dark enough.

3. Spread colored sugar onto a plate or baking sheet until completely dry.

Optional: Sugar cubes are the classic tea party sweetener. Make your own by combining ½ cup of your colored sugar with a small amount of water to make a crumbly paste. (Don't add too much, or the sugar will melt.) Press the sugar into small candy molds, and let dry overnight. Carefully remove the cubes, and serve.

Optional: For an extra twist, choose a mix-in for your sanding sugar. Coordinate with your signature sip's flavor!

* cocoa or vanilla bean powder
* finely crushed hard candy
* sprinkles
* edible glitter
* light sprinkle of Cayenne pepper, salt, or sour candy powder
* lemon, lime, or orange zest

13

PAMPER ME PRETTY

Why make a pricy trip to the spa? You can pamper with pals in the comfort of your own home!

THE LOOK

Comfort is the key! Tell your friends that the party is B.Y.O.B. (bring your own bathrobe.) Your friends will love lounging in their soft duds all day.

In-Style Invite

Hand out gift certificates for something great! Each certificate gives your guests entry to a super-exclusive spa–at your house! For an extra fun touch, do a creative spin on your last name and turn it into the "spa." Add a spa menu with all of the fun activities that your guests can look forward to taking part in.

Setting the Stage

Set the "me time" mood with scented candles, lots of floor pillows, and soothing music. Water pitchers and fresh fruit bowls will give your guests an extra-healthy punch.

Create various pampering stations. Each station should have different spa services your guests can indulge in. For the mani/pedi area, be sure to include nail art stickers, polishes, files, and buffers. A rose petal foot soak bowl is great for tired tootsies!

Eats and Treats

For food, focus on healthy bites such as cucumber finger sandwiches, fruit salad, and lettuce wraps. For dessert, go cutesy with these adorable and bite-sized "polish puffs!"

- pastel food coloring
- water or milk
- marshmallows
- chocolate frosting
- chocolate chews

Add food coloring to water or milk. Stir until food coloring is dissolved. Dip marshmallows into the colored liquid. Let dry. Dab some frosting onto one end of a chocolate chew. Press the frosting end into the center of each marshmallow so that it looks like a nail polish bottle. Arrange all of your puffs on a pretty platter and enjoy!

*Tip: For richer colors, dip the marshmallows into thinned frosting or candy melts.

Recipe: Foodie Facials

This makes a face mask good enough to eat!

- ⅓ cup (80 mL) cocoa powder
- ¼ cup (60 mL) raw honey
- 2 tablespoons (30 mL) mashed avocado

Combine all ingredients in a small bowl. Stir until creamy. Apply to the face for 15 minutes. Be sure to take pictures of everyone as masked mamas! Rinse with warm water. Make sure each guest has a towel for drying off.

Favors with Flair:

- handmade soaps
- flip-flops
- bottles of nail polish
- sleep masks

Signature Sip: All That Razz

Fruit-infused water is all the rage at fancy spas. One sip of this refreshing raspberry mocktail and you'll be saying, "Spaaahhh!"

- sparkling water (plain or flavored)
- fresh raspberries
- sliced lemon

Pour water into a glass. Add up to six fresh raspberries and garnish with a slice of lemon. You can also buy a glass cooler and have your guests help themselves.

YOU'VE GOT GAME

Host a makeshift massage studio by having everyone stand in a circle. Each girl rubs the shoulders of the girl in front of her. Operation: relaxation in progress!

TEA TIME

Why have tea for two when you can sip with a set of friends? Tip your pinky to this simply fabulous tea party!

THE LOOK

Pretty in pastel is the name of the game. Explore floral prints, elegant brooches, and strands of pearls. Ladylike looks are what tea party chic is all about. Give your guests white glove service with–what else?–white gloves!

In-Style Invite

Set the theme with teapot-shaped invitations. Choose classically girly patterns such as stripes, polka dots, flowers, and scallops.

Setting the Stage

Weather permitting, host your tea party outside in the backyard–ideally in the garden! Being outdoors will add an airy, festive feel.

Create a make-your-own-tea station where your besties can find their favorite flavor. Stock up on must-have tea blends such as jasmine, Earl Grey, herbal, and green.

Collect colorful teapots or dainty teacups to use as the table centerpieces. Set out place cards with your guests' names written in calligraphy.

Signature Sip: Honey Child

Not everyone loves hot tea, so why not offer something on the chill side too?

- ½ cup (120 mL) chilled green tea with honey and ginseng
- ¼ cup (60 mL) orange juice
- ¼ cup (60 mL) pineapple juice
- ½ cup (120 mL) ginger ale

Mix all the ingredients together. Serve over crushed ice for a refreshing beverage.

Favors with Flair:

- a variety of tea bags in a colorful sheer pouch
- lace frosted-glass tealight holders

YOU'VE GOT GAME

In Great Britain, high-styling Brits go out wearing funky hats called fascinators. Take a tip from the royals and have a fascinator-making contest! Set out elastic headbands, fabric glue, feathers, buttons, and other fun accessories. Whoever makes the most royally regal hat takes home a prize! Prize idea—the book *Tea with Jane Austen.*

Eats and Treats

Along with scones, pastries, and fresh fruit, finger sandwiches are absolutely a tea party must.

- cookie cutters
- white or wheat bread
- 1 pound (455 grams) of prepared chicken salad
- radish, thinly sliced
- cucumber, thinly sliced

Start by using cookie cutters to cut the bread into fun shapes, such as hearts, triangles, or stars. To make an open-face tea sandwich, spread chicken salad onto a piece of cut bread. Top with a thin slice of radish and cucumber. For extra decoration, use a small cookie cutter to decorate the sandwiches with tiny cucumber hearts and flowers.

Good Clean Fun

Who doesn't love suds? Your spa party will never fizzle with these surprising handmade soaps.

- scissors
- natural loofah
- round soap mold
- 1 pound (455 grams) melt and pour soap base
- microwave-safe bowl
- blue soap dye
- fragrance oil
- spray bottle
- rubbing alcohol
- plastic wrap

1. Cut the loofah into pieces small enough to fit into your soap mold. Set aside.

2. Cut the soap base into small cubes. Place in a microwave-safe container and heat until melted. Watch container carefully to make sure that the base does not boil over.

3. Add a drop of soap dye to the base. Continue adding dye until desired shade is reached.

4. Add fragrance oil. Stir until clear.

5. Place a piece of loofah into each soap mold.

6. Pour base into the molds. Spray the base with rubbing alcohol. The alcohol will remove any bubbles that rise to the surface.

7. Let soap harden at least three hours. Remove from the molds, and cover with plastic wrap.

Dress It Up

Plastic wrap will protect your soap from drying out, but it's not the prettiest packaging. Dress up your soaps to complete your pampering party.

- Use a tulle favor bag. Thread a bead or small charm onto the ribbon that ties the bag shut.

- Cover each bar in wrapping paper. Then decorate the bar with ribbon or raffia.

- Nestle soap in Chinese take-out boxes packed with tissue paper or colored shredded paper.

Feeling Festive

Psst! Want to know the trick to planning a party that truly stands out from the rest? Answer: truly creative thinking. There are a few quick tricks for transforming your party into something totally you-nique.

- Fill balloons with confetti or stars for a glitter-rific effect; you can also buy or make sequined candles for that extra special sparkle. Extra-large balloons also add a major "wow" factor.

- Rather than using a traditional wreath on the door, hang a colorful rainbow tutu! You're sure to get tons of compliments about your style being on pointe.

- Give ordinary food a special twist. Take time to create foods that fit your theme. Think out of the box and try making eats from scratch. Little touches, such as garnishes, favors, or servingware, really help your party stand out.

- Go big or go home! Get creative with cookie cutters, washi tape, food coloring, paper crafts, and printables. These simple and inexpensive items can really amp up your party theme.

- Go out of your way to let guests know you're thinking about them. Make sure anyone on a special diet will get enough to eat. Avoid anything that might cause an allergic reaction, such as nut products or latex balloons. Tailor favors to suit each guest's favorite colors or styles.

Earn Your Stripes

You've learned how to make layered drinks and colored ice cubes. Now combine the two to make a striped cube! Choose juices of different shades and lemonades that would go well together taste-wise. Create the layers by filling ice cube trays about one-third of the way full. Freeze completely. Repeat with two other liquids until the tray is full. Serve in sparkling water.

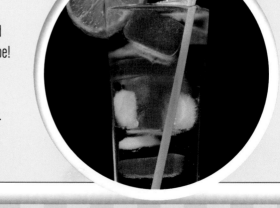

Putting the "Super" in Supervision

Having parents around doesn't equal no fun. Though it may seem somewhat uncool to have adults hanging around, trust that you'll be grateful they were there. To help supervision go as smoothly as possible, study strategies for success.

- [ ] Review plans for the party together the day before.

- [ ] Agree on a plan for what to do if uninvited guests find their way in.

- [ ] Go over the ground rules, such as leaving the lights on and keeping certain rooms off-limits. Be sure to discuss what will happen if someone breaks a rule.

- [ ] Agree on when your parents will be present and when they'll let you and your friends do your own thing.

- [ ] What will happen if there's an emergency? Having a plan in place will help for those just-in-case moments.

- [ ] Divvy up the workload and decide who will do what. Some parents find that serving food and drink throughout the party helps them be present without hovering.

- [ ] Don't forget about the parents of your guests. Get familiar with their rules before the party begins. If a guest's parents aren't OK with her wearing nail polish, make sure you have something else for her to do at your spa party.

- [ ] Remember, it's their house too. Be willing to make compromises about who will be where and when.

It's all about figuring out a system that works for you and your family. You'll be glad you did!

Don't forget to thank your parents after the party is over. You don't have to send them a thank-you note, but be sure to let them know you had a great time!

Hostess with the Mostest: Do's & Don'ts

Rolling out the welcome mat for your guests means going the extra mile to meet their needs. Here are some small things you can do that will make a big difference!

Do work ahead of time—whether that means setting the tables the day before or putting party favors in bags throughout the week. Getting as much prep work as possible done early will help you feel less frazzled the day of your big 'do!

Don't skimp on food and drink. Running out of these necessities can be a major prob! For a three-hour party, experts suggest having enough beverages for about three drinks per person. For appetizers, figure that each person might eat four to six bites per hour.

Do your best to make everyone feel welcome. Make sure you get to talk to each guest personally at some point during the party. And don't let them sneak out without saying good-bye!

Don't let your guests go hungry! At the beginning of the party, set out small bowls of nuts and other easy nibbles to tide people over until the food is ready. Nothing makes a party go downhill faster than hungry guests.

Do stay relaxed and have a blast. Some hostesses get so busy that they forget to have fun! Put that at the top of your priority list, and you'll be good to go.

Parties are the perfect place for all the people in your life to intersect. If you've invited different groups—school, sports, neighbors—make sure to introduce everyone. Try to find things your guests have in common to help them mingle. If you see someone not talking to anyone, put in special effort to make him or her feel at ease.

Take a read on your guests' mood and energy and be willing to be flexible. The perfect party you planned in your head might not be the one that's best for your guests. If they're not feeling a game or activity, just move on to something different. It's all about going with the flow!

Little Things Mean a Lot

Make a "just in case" basket in the bathroom. Include dental floss, lotion, lip balm, hairspray, and other personal items guests may need.

Tiny Treats: Favors That Rock

Favors are a way to send your guests home with a small memento of your party. They can be simple things that can be eaten or used right away. Or they can be objects guests will treasure for years to come.

Wrap candy or small trinkets, such as jewelry or toys, in tulle. (Homemade sugar cubes work perfectly here!) Tie the tulle with colorful ribbons and decorate with a special charm.

Personalize mini jars of jam with fabric and string. Choosing fun fabrics and colors will make your favor that much sweeter! Coordinating satchets of tea or a favorite scone recipe are nice touches too.

Make whimsical bubble wands by mixing ½ cup (120 mL) dishwashing liquid, 2 cups (480 mL) water, 2 teaspoons (10 mL) sugar, glitter, and food coloring. Divide bubble mix into small containers with bubble wands.

TIP: A few drops of glycerin will help make stronger bubbles. A few drops of essential oil will add a nice scent.

Give "green" a new meaning with tiny trees. Send each guest home with a seedling to plant in their own yard. They'll remember your party for years to come.

Find origami patterns that match your party theme. Give your guests their own origami figure, such as a tiny tea cup or a box to hold homemade soap. Or, better yet, send them home with origami paper and instructions on how to fold their own!

Nifty Nails

Leave a lasting impression with pretty polish! Let your guests go wild creating their own custom polishes.

- powdered eye shadows
- toothpick
- 3-inch (7.5-centimeter) square pieces of parchment paper
- clear nail polish
- glitter (optional)
- 4.5-millimeter ball bearings

1. Select your desired shade(s) of eye shadow. Use the toothpick to scrape eye shadow onto a piece of parchment paper.

2. Press the eye shadow between two pieces of parchment paper to grind into a fine powder.

3. Roll the parchment paper into a tight funnel. Use it to pour the eye shadow powder into the polish bottle.

4. Use a toothpick to stir the eye shadow into the polish.

5. Add glitter, if desired.

6. Add two or three ball bearings to the bottle. The ball bearings will help the polish mix evenly before each use.

FOR MORE CUSTOMIZATION, TRY:

- adding a drop or two of fragrance oil or food flavorings, such as vanilla, cinnamon, or orange. Your nails will look and smell great!

- using shaped glitter that matches your party theme.

- using a label-making program to design custom labels for your polish bottles.

- using food coloring instead of eye shadow for a neon effect. (Use a clear base coat before applying, to avoid staining your fingers.)

Lovely Lace

Use your new polish to give your nails a lacy look.

1. Paint the bottom half of each finger at an angle.

2. Use a toothpick to create scalloped patterns along the top edge of the polish.

3. Accent the tip of your nail with silver polish.

4. Finish with clear nail polish.

What's Next?

From planning to prep to party time, you've been on a pretty fantastic voyage! Congrats on a job well done—you've made the grade and earned an "A" in the art of being a hostess. Your next mission, should you choose to accept it? Pick a different theme and do it all over again! And take a deep breath: this book is here to show you the way.

PARTY PREP IN REVIEW

Choose a date!
Set time, place, budget, guest list, menu, party theme, and other important details.

Invite people!
Choose a guest list and send out invites.

Talk it over!
Discuss ground rules and supervision with parents or guardians. Have a plan in place for "what ifs."

Plan ahead!
Plan shopping lists and menus, favors, games, activities, and other party aspects. Practice recipes ahead of time and think about how they will be served and stored.

Clean, clean, clean!
Do a before and after cleaning of your party space. It's always nice to leave a space neater than the way you found it!

Viva la Celebration!

☐ **Make it yours!**
Customize decorations and other party pieces to fit your style and theme. Have fun with favors, food, and beverages to turn a party into your party.

☐ **Engage your guests!**
Your guests are there to have a good time. Make sure everyone is eating, drinking, and being merry!

☐ **Have a great time!**
Take a moment to relax and enjoy yourself! Taste the food, talk to your friends, and don't sweat the small stuff.

☐ **Tie up any loose strings.**
Clean up, send out thank-yous, and start planning for the next perfect party!

Read More

Beery, Barbara. *Barbara Beery's Pink Princess Party Cookbook.* New York: Simon & Schuster Books for Young Readers, 2011.

Blake, Susannah. *Crafts for Pampering Yourself.* Eco Chic. Berkeley Heights, N.J.: Enslow Publishers, Inc., 2013.

Kenney, Karen Latchana. *Cool Slumber Parties: Perfect Party Planning for Kids.* Cool Parties. Minneapolis: ABDO Publishing Company, 2012.

Internet Sites

FactHound offers a safe, fun way to find Internet sites related to this book. All of the sites on FactHound have been researched by our staff.

Here's all you do:

Visit *www.facthound.com*

Type in this code: 9781476540085

Check out projects, games and lots more at **www.capstonekids.com**